# Collins

## My First Book of

# The
# Human Body

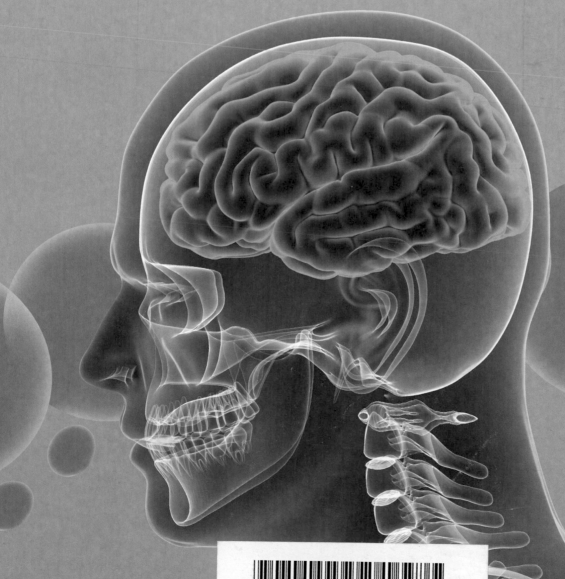

**Collins My First Book of
The Human Body**
Collins
An imprint of HarperCollins Publishers
Westerhill Road
Bishopbriggs
Glasgow
G64 2QT

First edition 2011
Second edition 2013

Copyright © Q2AMEDIA 2011

ISBN 978-0-00-752115-9

Imp 001

Collins® is a registered trademark of

HarperCollins Publishers Limited
www.collinslanguage.com
A catalogue record for this book is available from the British Library

Printed by South China Printing Company, China

**Author:** Jen Green
**Editor:** Jean Coppendale
**Project Manager:** Shekhar Kapur
**Art Director:** Joita Das
**Designers:** Ankita Sharma, Jasmeen Kaur, Kanika Kohli and Souvik Mukherjee
**Picture Researchers:** Akansha Srivastava and Saloni Vaid

**For the Publisher:**
Elaine Higgleton
Ruth O'Donovan

**Managing Editor:** Alysoun Owen
**Editor:** Jill Laidlaw

# Collins

## My First Book of

# The
# Human Body

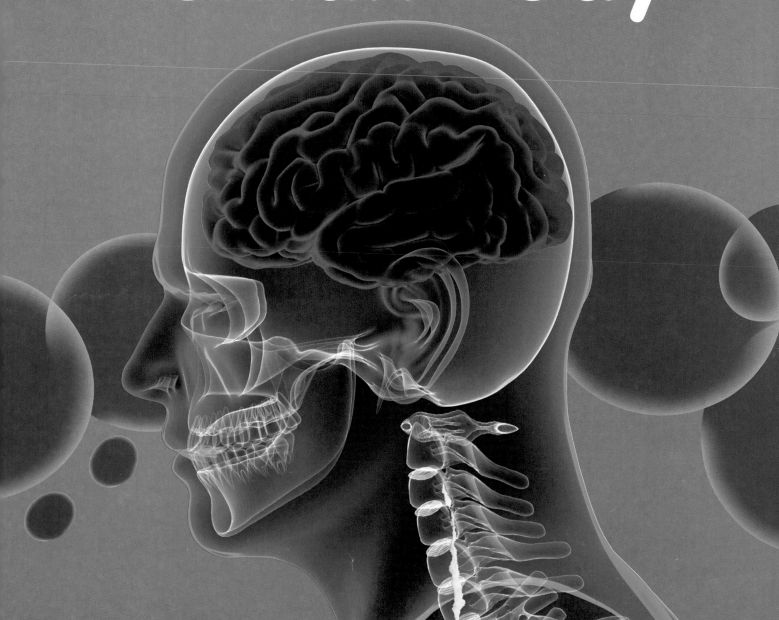

# Contents

# Your Amazing Body

The human body is an amazing living machine. Inside your body there are millions of parts working together to keep you healthy and active. This book looks at how our bodies are built and how they work. No two people look exactly the same on the outside, but the insides of our bodies are all very much alike.

We all look different on the outside but have the same working parts inside, such as a brain, heart, lungs and kidneys.

Senses such as sight and touch help you to read and write.

Your body is made up of millions of tiny parts called cells.

Your brain and nervous system help you balance.

# Brain and Nerves

Your brain is like an amazing machine and is more complicated than any computer. It allows you to think and move, and keeps your body working well. Your brain controls your actions, using a network of nerves that stretches throughout your body.

## What is your brain made of?

Your body is made of tiny parts called cells. You have many different types of cells, such as heart cells and blood cells. Your body contains millions and millions of cells. Your brain is made up of tiny nerve cells. These cells have spider-like arms, which connect with other nerve cells.

When you think, tiny electrical signals flash between your brain cells.

# Learning

Thanks to your brain, you can carry out all sorts of complicated actions, from riding a bike to playing a musical instrument. Your brain also helps you to learn new things.

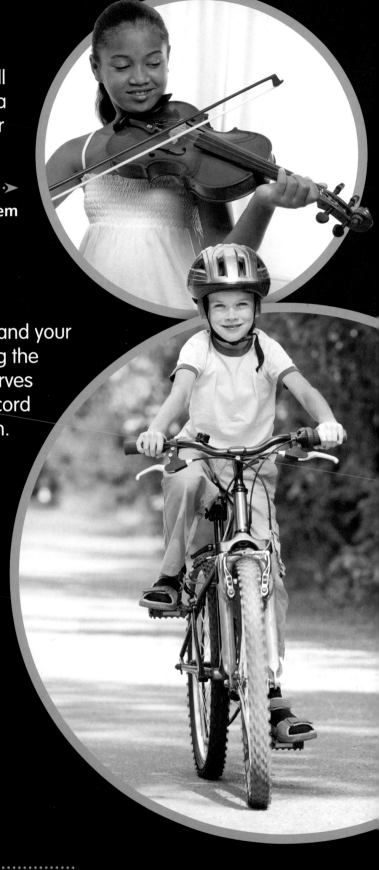

**Your brain and nervous system help you to play the violin.**

# Nervous system

Nerves carry signals between your brain and your body. Most of these messages pass along the spinal cord, which is a large bundle of nerves in your body. Together your brain, spinal cord and nerves make up your nervous system.

**Your nervous system helps you keep steady on a bike.**

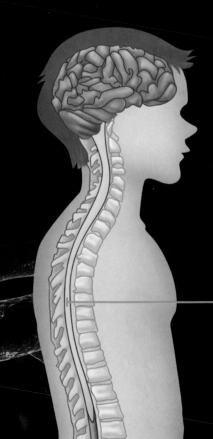

**Spinal cord**

**Your spinal cord stretches from the bottom of your brain to your lower back.**

9

# Control Centre

Your brain is the control centre of your body. It allows you to think, learn and to solve problems. It keeps the different parts of your body working smoothly, even when you are asleep. Feelings and thoughts happen in your brain. Memories are stored there, too.

## Brain case

Your brain is a soft, spongy organ in your head. The surface of your brain is very wrinkly. Your skull is a hard case that protects your brain, like a crash helmet. Your hair and the skin on your head also help to protect your brain.

←.............................

**Your delicate brain is protected by your hair, skin and skull.**

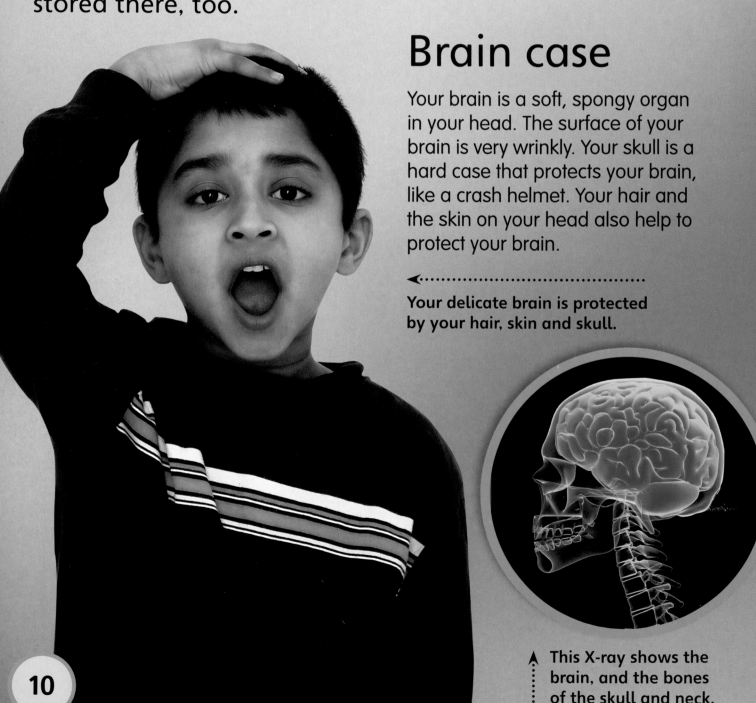

**This X-ray shows the brain, and the bones of the skull and neck.**

# Cerebrum and cerebellum

Your brain has three main parts: the cerebrum, cerebellum and brain stem. The cerebrum is the top part of your brain. You use it to think, remember and to order your body to move. The cerebellum helps you to balance and keeps your muscles working smoothly.

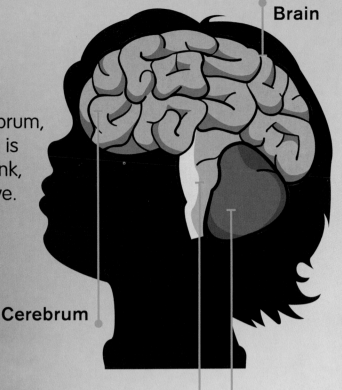

Brain

Cerebrum

Brain stem

Cerebellum

Brain stem

◀┄┄┄┄┄┄┄┄┄┄┄

**When you run, your brain stem tells your lungs and heart to work harder.**

# Brain stem

The brain stem is the bottom part of the brain, and connects with the spinal cord. It controls things your body does automatically (without thinking), such as breathing and digestion.

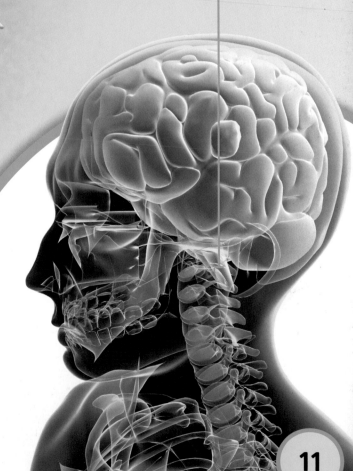

# Nerve Network

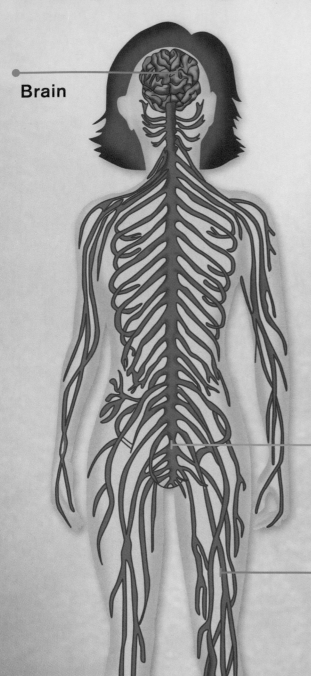

Brain

Spinal cord

Nerves

A network of nerves reaches every part of your body. Messages travel along it at high speed to tell your brain about your surroundings. Quick as a flash, your brain sends a message back along the nerve network, telling your body to move in certain ways.

This picture shows the spinal cord and main nerves in your body.

## Longest nerve

The sciatic nerve is the longest nerve in your body. It stretches all the way from the base of your spine to your toes.

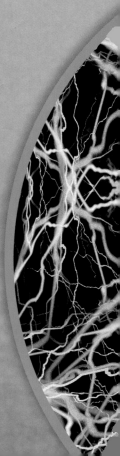

# Spinal cord

Your spinal cord is made up of a bundle of nerves. It is about as thick as your finger. It runs down inside the knobbly bones of your spine. These bones protect your spinal cord from injury, just as your skull protects your brain.

The bones that protect your spinal cord are called vertebrae. Your spine has 26 vertebrae in all.

The thread-like things in this photograph are nerves.

## Vertebrae

Spine

Spinal cord

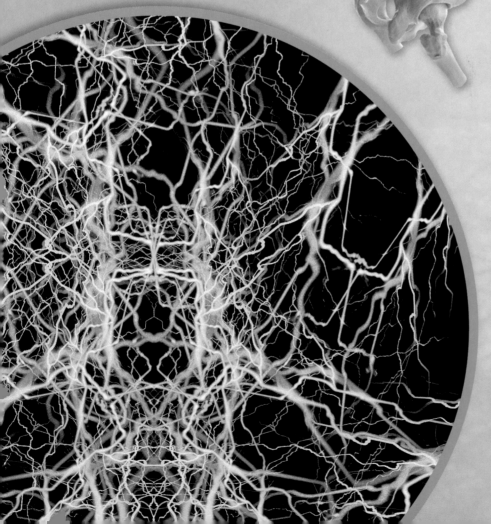

# What are nerves?

Nerve cells link together to make long threads called nerves. There are two main types of nerves. Sensory nerves send information from your senses to your brain. Motor nerves send signals from your brain to your muscles, telling them to move.

# How the Brain Works

How do you learn and remember things? Is your brain always in control of your actions? What happens to your brain when you sleep? These tricky questions have puzzled us for many years, but scientists now think they have the answers.

## Learning and memory

Your brain is a mass of nerve cells all linked together. As you learn something, messages flash along some of these nerves, and they become like well-worn pathways. As you use these paths more often, it gets easier for the messages to flash along.

**Do you remember when you learned to ride a bike? At first it was very hard, but with practice it became easier.**

# Reflex actions

Sometimes, your body reacts very quickly to save you from danger. If you touch something very hot, pain sensors in your fingers send a signal towards your brain. When this message reaches your spinal cord, it sends a signal back to move your hand away. All this happens so fast that the message doesn't even reach your brain. This is called a reflex action.

**A reflex action jerks your finger away if you touch a cactus spine.**

# Sleep and dreams

When you are asleep, your brain is still busy. This activity is called dreaming. Experts believe that dreams are the brain's way of sorting through things that have happened during the day.

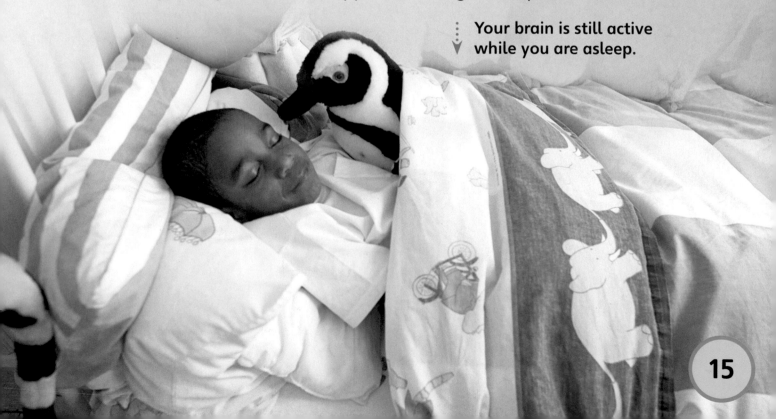

**Your brain is still active while you are asleep.**

# Bones and Muscles

Bones and muscles give your body its shape and allow it to move. Without bones, you would collapse in a floppy heap on the ground. Without muscles, you wouldn't be able to move at all.

Muscles allow you to carry out hundreds of different movements, such as crouching, sitting, standing, running and playing different sports.

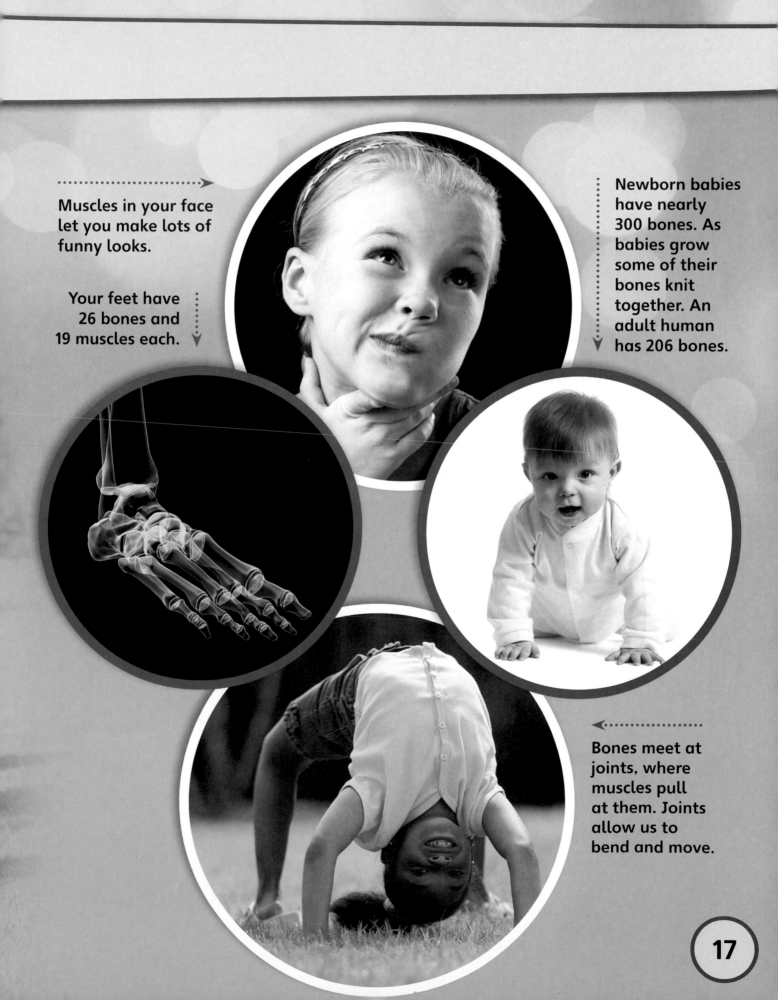

Muscles in your face let you make lots of funny looks.

Your feet have 26 bones and 19 muscles each.

Newborn babies have nearly 300 bones. As babies grow some of their bones knit together. An adult human has 206 bones.

Bones meet at joints, where muscles pull at them. Joints allow us to bend and move.

# Skeleton

All the bones in your body are linked to your skeleton by muscles and stringy tendons. You are the shape you are because of your skeleton.

## Your skeleton

Your skeleton and bones protect your organs such as your brain and heart. Every bone in your body has an ordinary name and a scientific one, which is used by doctors. For example, the thigh bone is also called the femur.

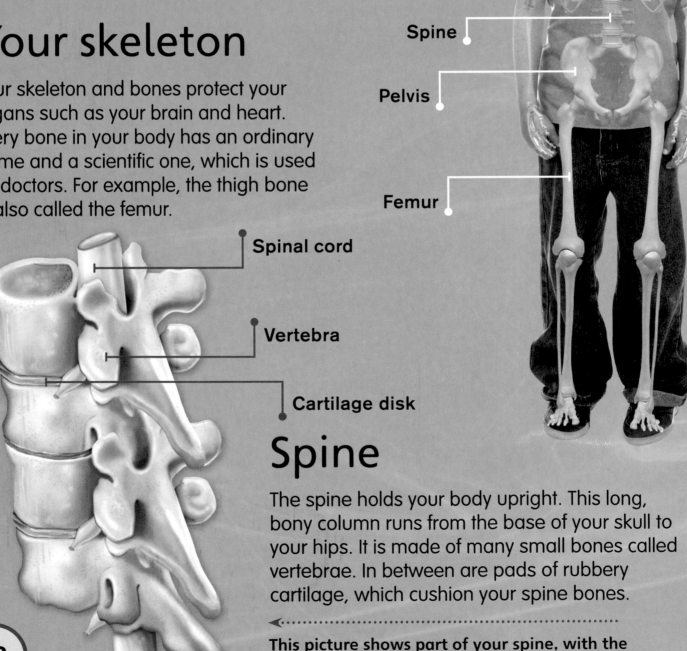

Skull

Humerus

Ribcage

Spine

Pelvis

Femur

Spinal cord

Vertebra

Cartilage disk

## Spine

The spine holds your body upright. This long, bony column runs from the base of your skull to your hips. It is made of many small bones called vertebrae. In between are pads of rubbery cartilage, which cushion your spine bones.

This picture shows part of your spine, with the spinal cord running inside the knobbly bones.

# Hands and feet

Your hand and wrist contain 27 bones. All these little bones allow you to grip objects as small as a needle or as large as a beach ball. You can also point, throw, catch and make a fist. Your feet have 26 bones each. The bones in your hands and feet make up more than half of all the bones in your body.

The delicate bones in your hands allow you to catch a beachball.

# Ribcage

Your ribs are attached to your spine. Your ribs curve around to form a bony frame called the ribcage. This protects the soft organs inside, such as your lungs and liver.

Your ribcage has 12 pairs of ribs. Together they protect your vital inner organs.

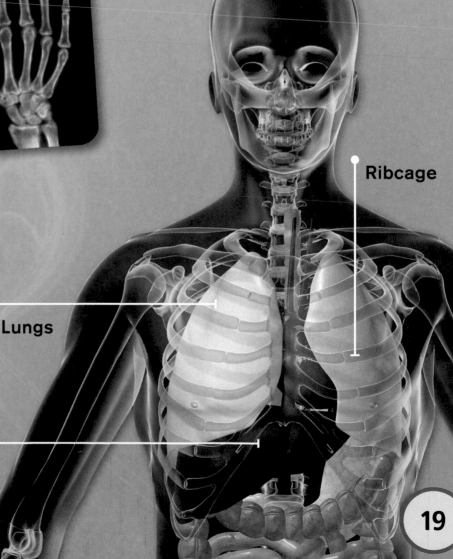

Ribcage

Lungs

Liver

# Bones

Bones are light but very strong. The bones inside you are alive, unlike the dry, dead bones you see in museums. Like other body parts, they have nerves and blood vessels. Living bones grow and change like the rest of you as you grow up.

## What are bones like inside?

Bones have several layers. The outer layer is very hard. Inside is a softer layer filled with holes, like a bath sponge. In the centre, there is a space filled with jelly called bone marrow. Many of your blood cells are made here.

**Hard outer bone**

**Spongy bone**

**Bone marrow**

Your bones are made of different layers. This makes them strong and allows them to flex slightly.

# Cartilage

Your ears and nose are stiffened (made firm) not with bone but with gristly cartilage. This rubbery material makes them flexible (bendy). Before you were born, all your bones were made of cartilage. Later, this cartilage slowly hardened into bone.

Cartilage makes your nose strong and bendy.

# Broken bones

Bones are very tough. But they can snap if they get a hard knock, or are badly twisted. Luckily, bones heal and knit back together quite quickly – often in less than two months. You usually wear a sling or a plaster cast to keep the bone in position while it heals.

Broken bones heal more quickly when you are young.

## Skull bone

The human skull has 22 bones. The only bone that moves in your skull is your jawbone – all the other bones are fixed.

# Joints

The places where bones meet are called joints. Different joints allow your arms, legs, neck and other body parts to move in different ways. Thanks to your joints, you can bend, twist, stretch and jump. What types of movement do you enjoy doing most of all? The main types of joints are shown on these two pages.

## Hinge joint

Hinge joints allow your bones to move in just one direction, like a door hinge. A hinge joint in your knee connects your leg bones. A hinge joint in your elbow connects your arm bones.

Hinge joints allow you to bend your knees and elbows.

Hinge joint

# Ball-and-socket joint

Ball-and-socket joints allow your limbs to move in many directions. A ball-and-socket joint connects your thigh bone with your hip bone. The thigh bone has a rounded end, which fits inside a hollow in the hip bone. A ball-and-socket joint in your shoulder allows you to swing your arms.

**The X-ray (right) shows the ball-and-socket joint in your shoulder.**

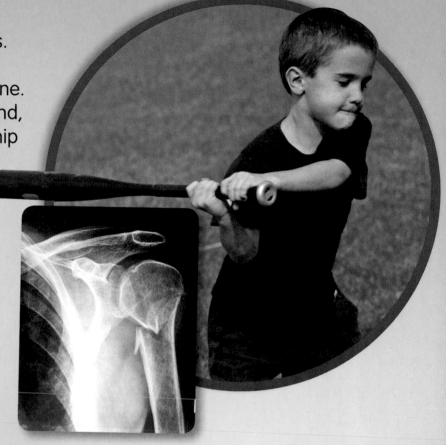

**The pivot joint in your neck allows you to move your head freely.**

# Pivot joint

Pivot joints allow your bones to swivel. A pivot joint in your neck lets you turn your head from side to side.

# Oiling the joints

Smooth, rubbery cartilage covers the ends of your bones. Joints contain a special fluid, which works like oil on a door hinge, to prevent rubbing. Strong straps called ligaments hold your bones in place at the joints.

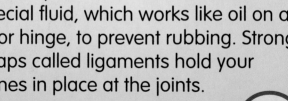

23

# Muscles

Muscles move every part of your body. You use the muscles fixed to your bones to sit, stand, run, dance and cycle. You also use muscles to breathe, digest your food and keep blood pumping around your body.

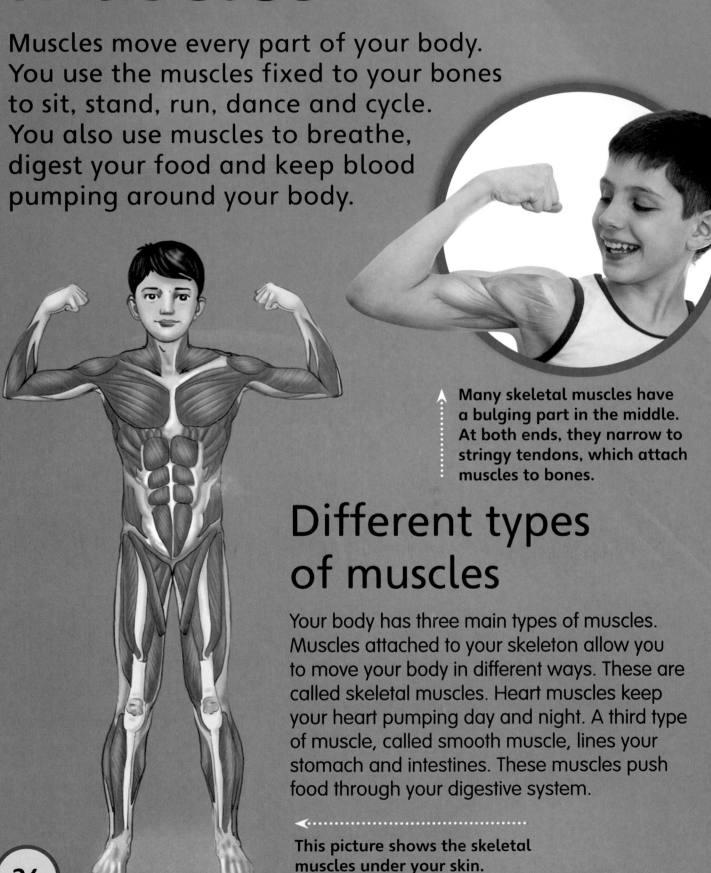

Many skeletal muscles have a bulging part in the middle. At both ends, they narrow to stringy tendons, which attach muscles to bones.

## Different types of muscles

Your body has three main types of muscles. Muscles attached to your skeleton allow you to move your body in different ways. These are called skeletal muscles. Heart muscles keep your heart pumping day and night. A third type of muscle, called smooth muscle, lines your stomach and intestines. These muscles push food through your digestive system.

This picture shows the skeletal muscles under your skin.

Small muscles in your eyes allow you to blink and wink. Tiny muscles in your fingers help you to do small actions, such as threading a needle.

# Inside a muscle

Muscles are bundles of long, stringy fibres. These muscle fibres are made of long muscle cells. Muscle cells do their work by contracting (getting shorter) to pull on bones.

Muscles come in different shapes and sizes. The big muscles in your legs and shoulders allow you to carry out big movements, such as kicking or throwing.

**Muscle cells**

**Muscle fibre**

# How Muscles Work

Muscles work by pulling on bones. When you want to move part of your body, your brain sends signals to certain muscles, telling them to shorten and then to relax. Hundreds of muscles work together when you carry out a difficult action, such as playing the recorder or touching your toes.

## Muscle pairs

Muscles can only pull on bones, they cannot push them. For this reason, muscles are arranged in pairs. One muscle pulls a bone one way. The other muscle then pulls it back again.

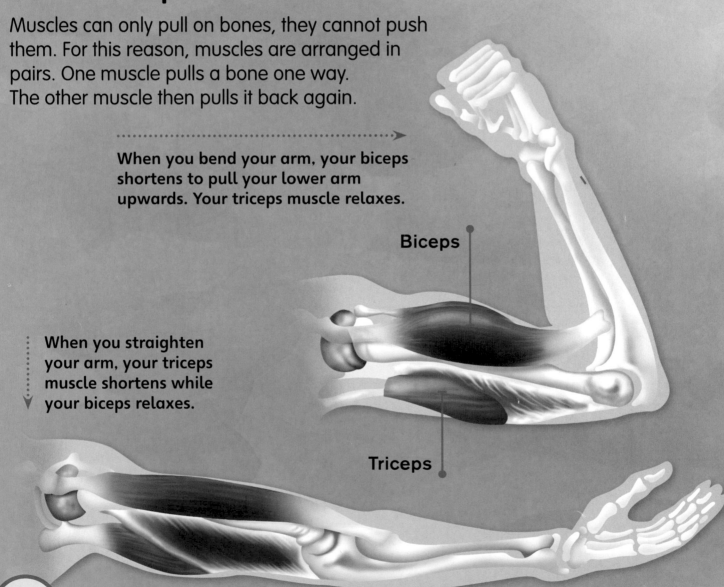

**When you bend your arm, your biceps shortens to pull your lower arm upwards. Your triceps muscle relaxes.**

**Biceps**

**When you straighten your arm, your triceps muscle shortens while your biceps relaxes.**

**Triceps**

# Feel your muscles working

Feel your biceps muscle. When a muscle contracts, it gets shorter and fatter. The muscle bulges. When it relaxes, it gets longer and thinner.

## Face muscles

Over 40 muscles in your face allow you to grin, frown and pull funny faces. Try pulling a funny face you have never made before!

If you flex your arm like this, you can feel your biceps muscle at the top of your upper arm.

Muscles in your face let you move your eyes, nose, cheeks and mouth.

## New skills

Can you pat the top of your head and rub your tummy at the same time? Your brain has to work out how to move your muscles for this new skill. It feels awkward at first, but soon becomes easier.

27

# Heart, Blood and Lungs

You need a gas called oxygen to live. Your heart, lungs and blood allow oxygen to reach every part of your body. Your brain needs oxygen to think. Your muscles need it to pull on bones, and your digestive system needs it to break down food. Every cell in your body needs oxygen to do its work.

Your heart and lungs work hard when you are running. You breathe harder and your heart beats faster to send enough oxygen to your blood and muscles.

This picture shows how air is breathed into your mouth, travels down your windpipe and goes into your lungs.

Your heart pumps oxygen-rich blood through your body. You can put a stethoscope to your chest to hear your heart doing its work.

Red blood cells carry oxygen to different parts of your body.

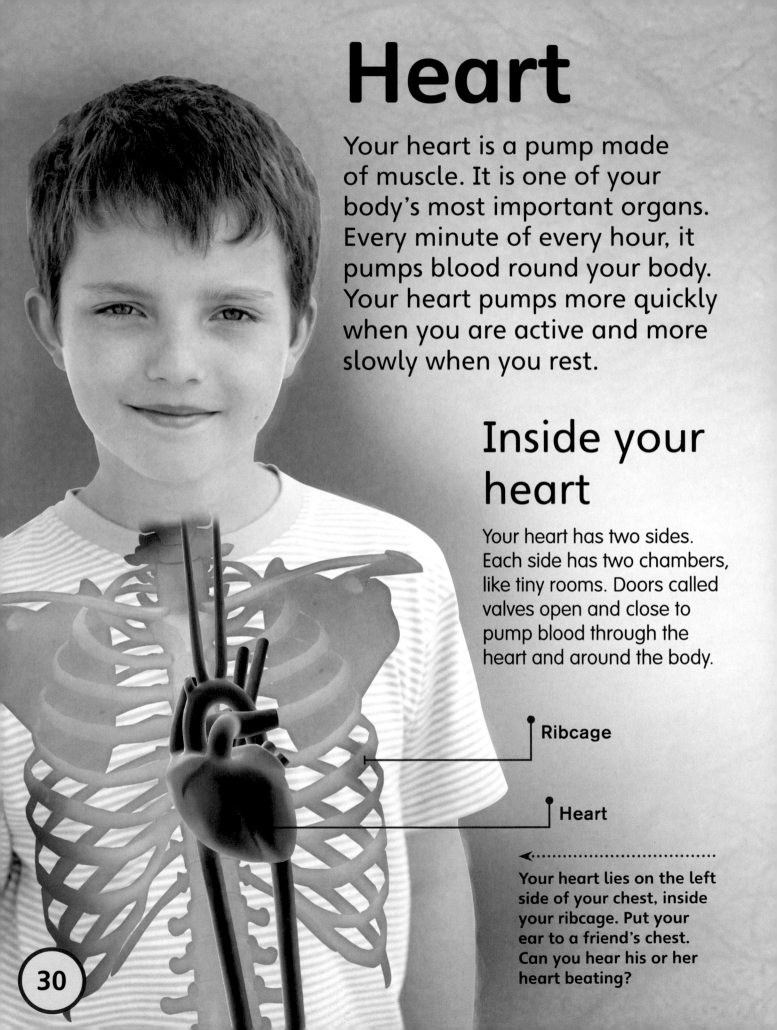

# Heart

Your heart is a pump made of muscle. It is one of your body's most important organs. Every minute of every hour, it pumps blood round your body. Your heart pumps more quickly when you are active and more slowly when you rest.

## Inside your heart

Your heart has two sides. Each side has two chambers, like tiny rooms. Doors called valves open and close to pump blood through the heart and around the body.

Ribcage

Heart

Your heart lies on the left side of your chest, inside your ribcage. Put your ear to a friend's chest. Can you hear his or her heart beating?

# Pumping station

Your heart is like two pumps in one. The right side of your heart pumps blood from your body to your lungs, where it collects oxygen. The left side pumps oxygen-rich blood from your lungs to the rest of your body.

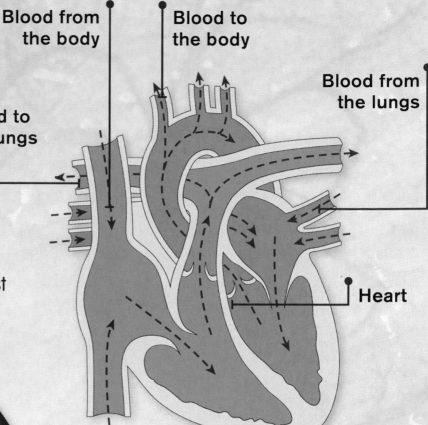

**Blood from the body**

**Blood to the body**

**Blood to the lungs**

**Blood from the lungs**

Heart

↑ Your heart pumps blood low in oxygen (shown in blue) to the lungs and oxygen-rich blood (shown in red) to the body.

When you exercise, your heart beats faster to pump blood to your muscles. Your heart also speeds up when you are feeling scared or excited.

# Your pulse

You can feel the beat of your heart as your blood surges through tubes called arteries. These little surges are called your pulse.

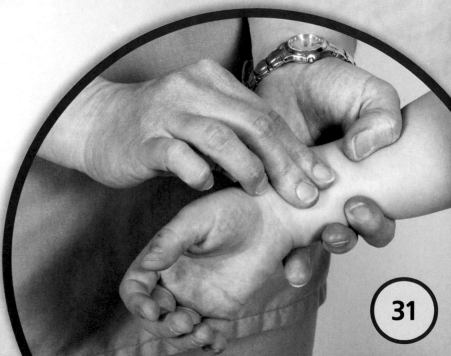

You can feel your pulse on the inside of your wrist.

31

# Blood

Blood is your body's transport system. It carries oxygen and nourishment (goodness) to every part of your body. Your blood also removes waste that could harm you. Your blood helps your body fight germs and mend cuts and grazes.

## What is blood made of?

Blood contains three types of cells, called white cells, red cells and platelets. These cells float in a watery liquid called plasma. The three types of cells and plasma all have different jobs to do.

This picture shows blood cells in plasma. Plasma helps carry nutrients, such as salts and sugars, to cells throughout your body.

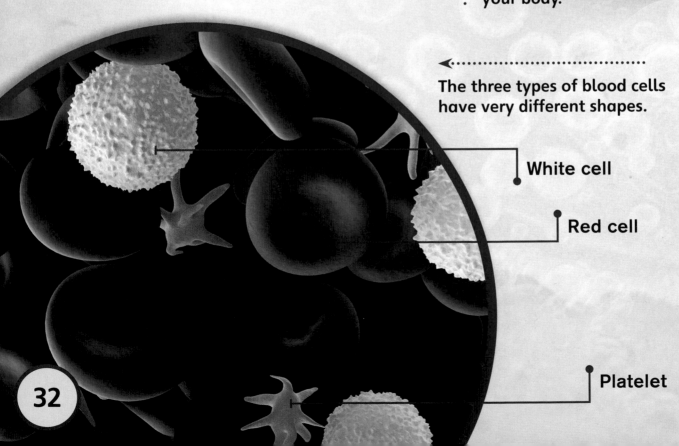

The three types of blood cells have very different shapes.

White cell

Red cell

Platelet

# Red blood cells

Red blood cells give your blood its colour. They are shaped like tiny doughnuts. These cells collect oxygen from your lungs and carry it around your body. They also collect and remove waste.

# White blood cells

White blood cells are larger than red cells. They help the body fight disease by destroying germs.

# Platelets

Platelets are tiny parts of cells that heal wounds. They also prevent you from bleeding too much.

# Cuts and clotting

If you cut yourself, platelets in your blood at the wound stick together to form a mesh. Red blood cells are trapped in this mesh and form a clot that seals the wound. The blood dries to form a scab. When the wound is healed, the scab falls off.

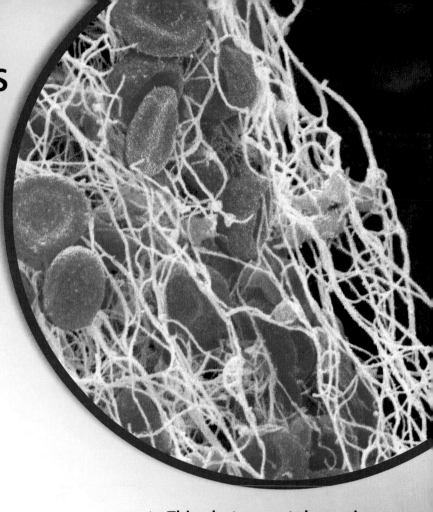

This photo was taken using a microscope. It shows red blood cells caught in a mesh of platelets at a wound.

Grazed skin forms a scab while the wound heals. The scab comes off when the skin has healed.

33

# Blood's Journey

Blood flows to every part of your body. From your heart, it travels to cells throughout your body and back again. It reaches your head and hands as well as your feet and toes. It flows in a circle and never stops moving. We call this movement "circulation".

**Arteries**

## Blood vessels

Blood flows through a network of tubes called blood vessels. There are three types of blood vessels. These are arteries, veins and capillaries.

Tubes called arteries carry oxygen-rich blood away from your heart to the rest of your body.

Tubes called veins carry used blood, which is low in oxygen, from your body back to your heart.

**Veins**

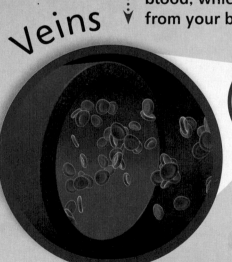

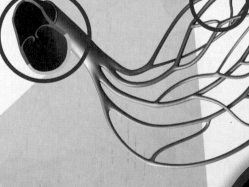

**Capillaries**

Very small tubes called capillaries carry oxygen-rich blood and nutrients to your cells. A network of fine capillaries link arteries and veins.

# Circulation

This diagram shows how blood circles through your body. Blood rich in oxygen is coloured red. Blood low in oxygen is coloured blue.

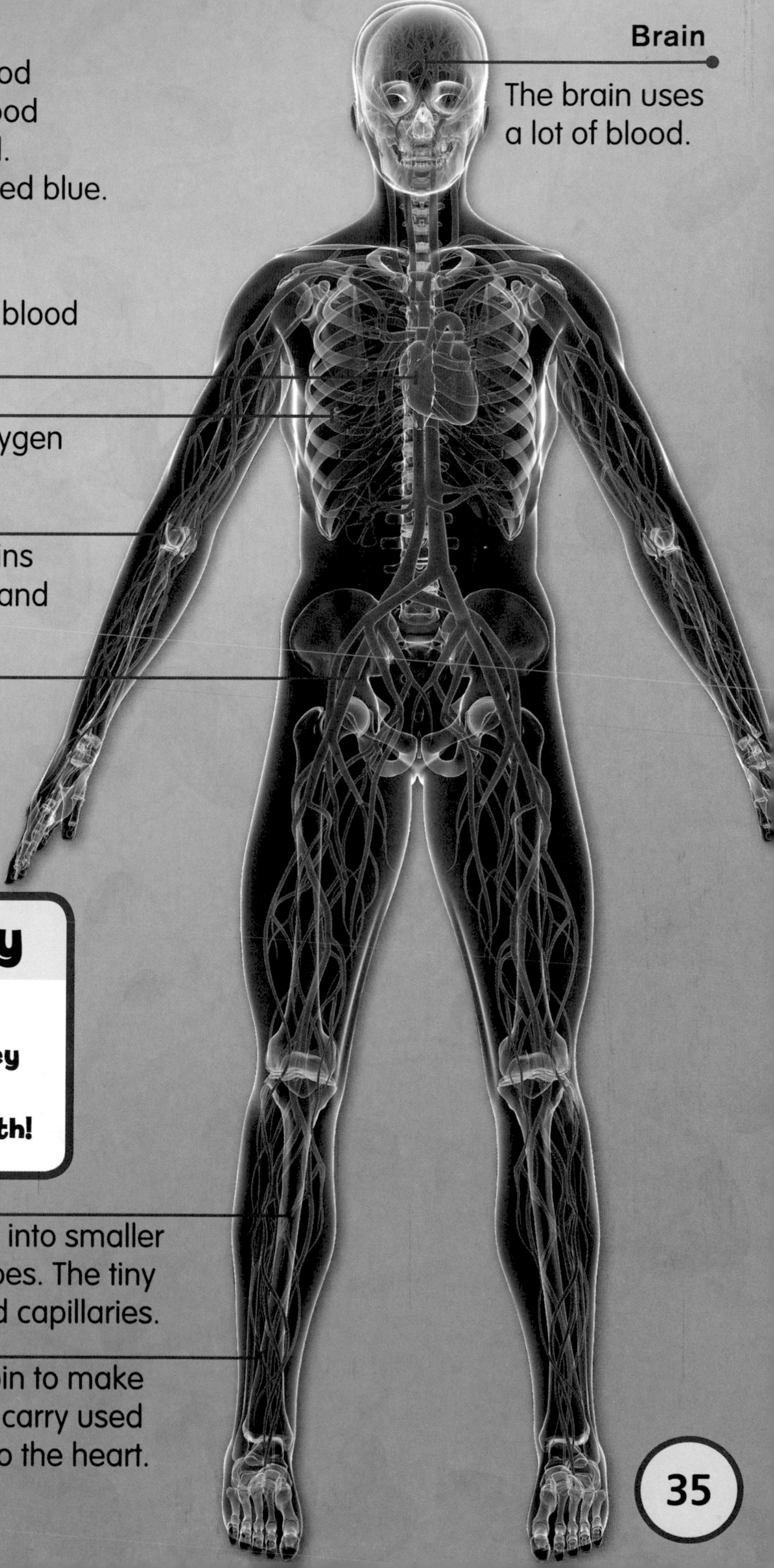

**Brain**
The brain uses a lot of blood.

**Heart** — The heart pumps blood around the body.

**Lungs** — Blood collects oxygen from the lungs.

**Veins** — Blood from the veins goes to the heart and then to the lungs.

**Kidneys** — Kidneys clean the blood and remove waste.

## A long journey

If all your blood vessels were laid end to end, they would stretch two and a half times round the Earth!

**Arteries** — Arteries branch into smaller and smaller tubes. The tiny tubes are called capillaries.

**Capillaries** — Capillaries join to make veins, which carry used blood back to the heart.

# Breathing

Every minute of every day, your body needs oxygen to work and to stay healthy. As you breathe in, your lungs take in air containing oxygen. You breathe out stale air containing the waste gas carbon dioxide, which your body does not want.

## Breathing muscles

You breathe using two sets of muscles. These are the muscles between your ribs, and a flat sheet of muscle below your lungs, called the diaphragm.

Your lungs are on the left and right side of your chest, inside your ribcage. Your left lung is smaller than your right lung, to make room for your heart.

## In and out

When you breathe in, your diaphragm drops down, and your rib muscles pull your ribs outwards. This sucks air into your lungs. When you breathe out, your diaphragm relaxes and moves upwards. Your rib muscles relax to bring the ribs in. This forces air out of your lungs.

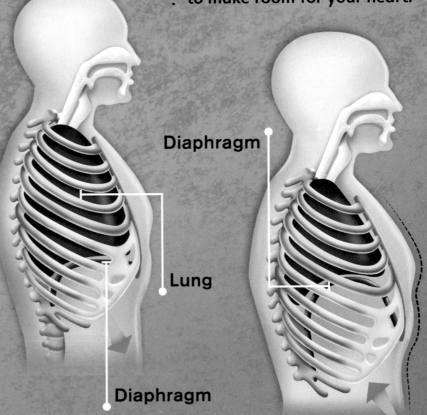

**Diaphragm**

**Lung**

**Diaphragm**

The diaphragm moves down and your ribs move out as you breathe in.

The diaphragm moves up and the ribs move in as you breathe out.

# Your airways

When you breathe in, air is sucked through your nostrils and mouth. It travels down your throat and windpipe to two pipes called bronchi. These branch into smaller and smaller pipes, which end in tiny air sacs.

This picture shows how your airways divide to form smaller and smaller pipes inside your lungs.

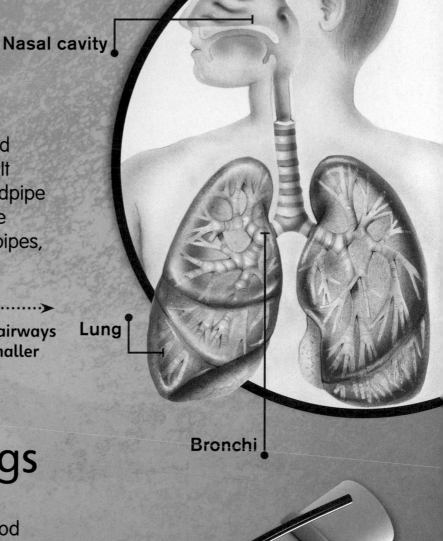

Nasal cavity

Lung

Bronchi

# Inside the lungs

The tiny air sacs in your lungs are surrounded by a mesh of fine blood vessels. Oxygen seeps through into the blood to flow to the rest of your body. Carbon dioxide in the blood passes into your lungs, so you can breathe it out.

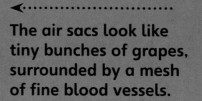

The air sacs look like tiny bunches of grapes, surrounded by a mesh of fine blood vessels.

# Making Sounds

When you breathe with your lungs, you are able to make sounds. You can make these sounds into words so you can talk to people. You also use breathing and sound when you sing, whistle, sigh, laugh and cry.

## Your voice box

You make sounds using the voice box near the top of your windpipe. Your voice box contains two flaps of skin, which are stretched by muscles. These are your vocal cords.

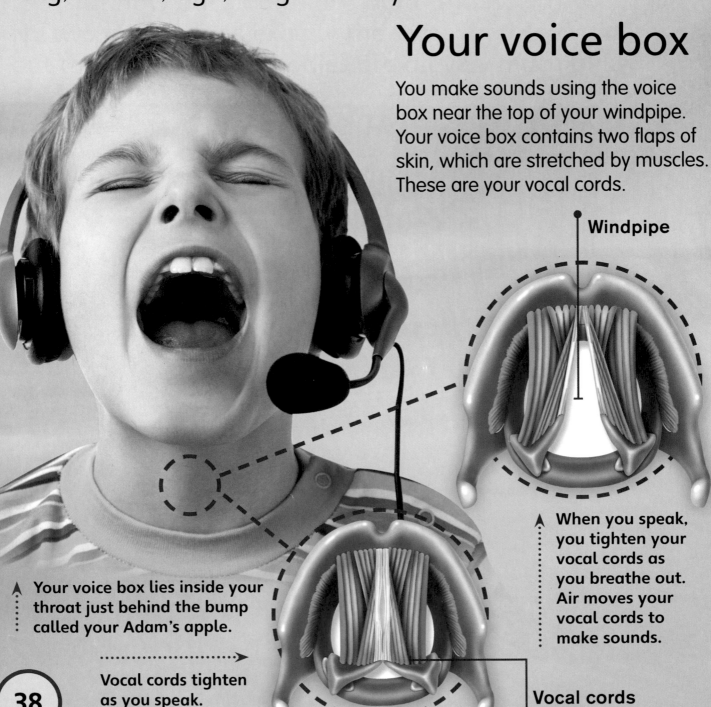

**Windpipe**

Your voice box lies inside your throat just behind the bump called your Adam's apple.

Vocal cords tighten as you speak.

When you speak, you tighten your vocal cords as you breathe out. Air moves your vocal cords to make sounds.

**Vocal cords**

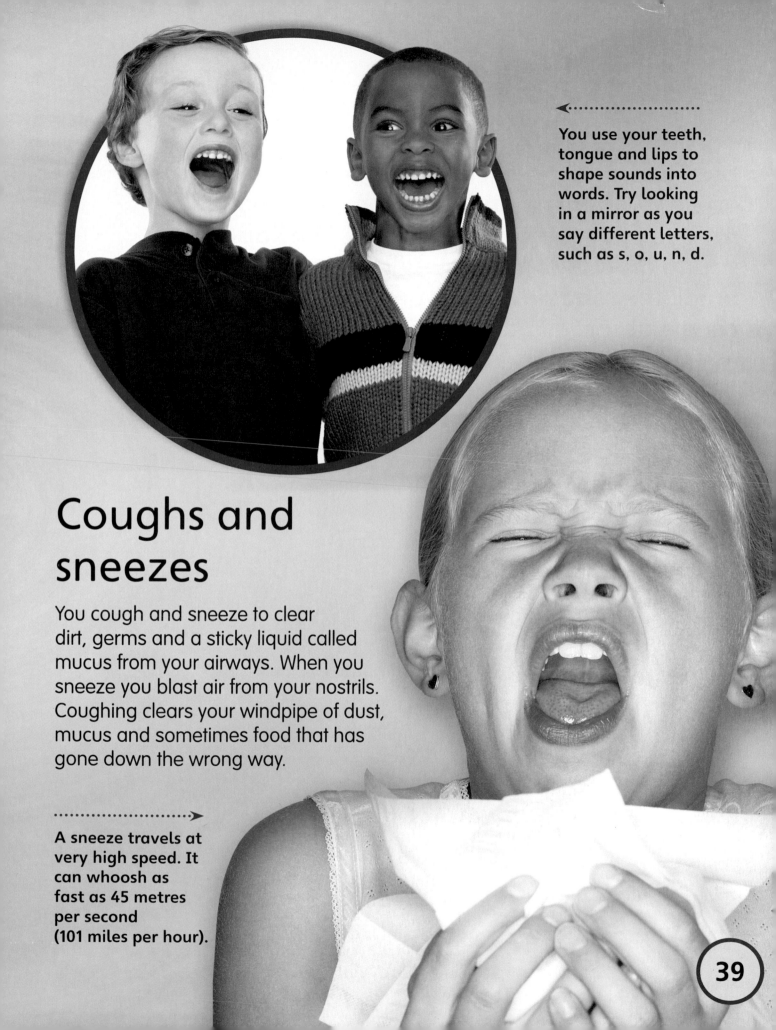

You use your teeth, tongue and lips to shape sounds into words. Try looking in a mirror as you say different letters, such as s, o, u, n, d.

# Coughs and sneezes

You cough and sneeze to clear dirt, germs and a sticky liquid called mucus from your airways. When you sneeze you blast air from your nostrils. Coughing clears your windpipe of dust, mucus and sometimes food that has gone down the wrong way.

A sneeze travels at very high speed. It can whoosh as fast as 45 metres per second (101 miles per hour).

# Digestion

Food provides the energy you need to keep you going. Nutrients (goodness) from your food are needed to repair cuts and grazes. They also help you to grow. But first, your digestive system must break the food down into tiny pieces, so that it can be absorbed and used.

You use your jaw muscles when chewing.

After you eat, food takes about a day to pass right through the digestive system.

Your stomach is about the size of an adult fist. It can stretch and become bigger when it is full.

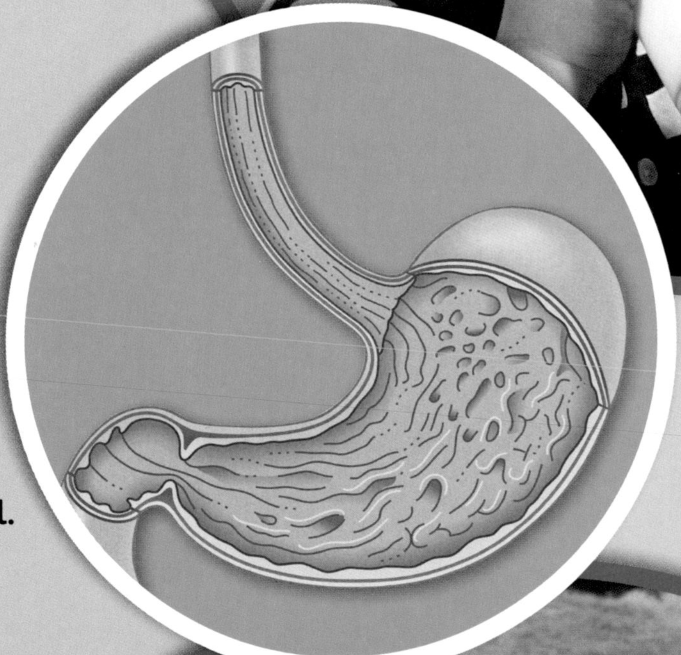

Food supplies the energy you need to play sport.

# Mouth

The work of digestion begins as soon as you put food into your mouth. While you enjoy tasting your food, your teeth, tongue and saliva start to turn hard or crunchy foods into soft, soggy lumps that you can swallow.

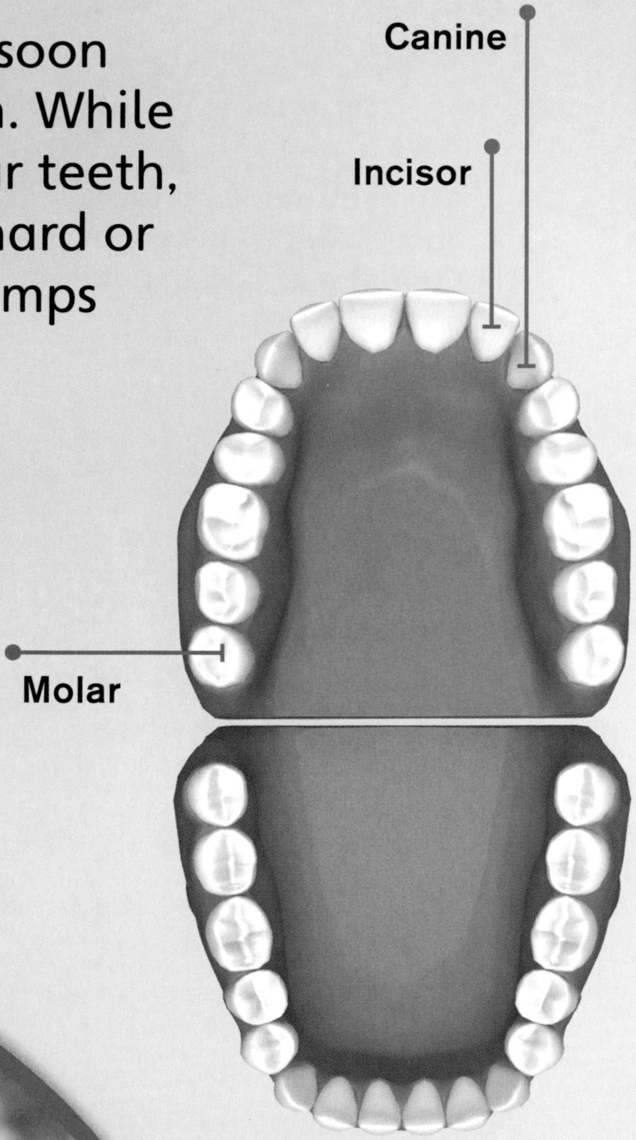

## Biting and chewing

Your teeth chop and mash food into small pieces. You have three main types of teeth, which do different jobs. Sharp front teeth called incisors bite and chop food. Pointed canines behind the incisors tear and rip. Broad back teeth called molars grind and mash food.

Canine

Incisor

Molar

Powerful jaw muscles allow you to bite into an apple or crusty bread.

# Parts of a tooth

The part of a tooth that you can see is called the crown. It is made of a very hard material called enamel. Below that is a softer layer called dentine. In the centre is a soft pulp containing nerves and blood vessels. The root fixes the tooth into your jaw.

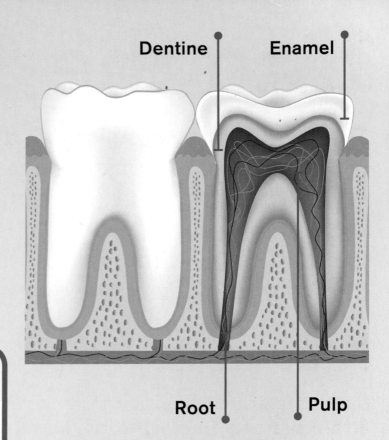

Dentine    Enamel

Root    Pulp

## Milk teeth

**Your first teeth are called your milk teeth. These started to grow when you were about six months old, when your main food was milk. When you are about six years old, these teeth start to drop out. They are replaced by your permanent, or adult, teeth.**

Take care of your teeth by brushing them at least twice a day. This removes bits of food that could decay in your mouth and harm your teeth.

# Tongue and saliva

As you chew, watery saliva mixes with your food to make it moist. Your tongue pushes the food against your teeth. When you have finished chewing, your tongue pushes the ball of soft food to the back of your mouth for swallowing.

# Into the Stomach

The food you swallow passes down your throat into your stomach. It stays here for up to five hours, while digestive juices break it down to make a thick soup. Your food is then ready to leave your stomach and pass to the intestines for the next stage of the digestive process.

## Food tube

The tube that carries food down to your stomach is called the oesophagus. This food tube lies next to your windpipe, that carries air to your lungs. As you swallow, a flap called the epiglottis at the top of your windpipe closes, so you do not choke.

Rings of muscles in the oesophagus tighten and relax to push food down your throat.

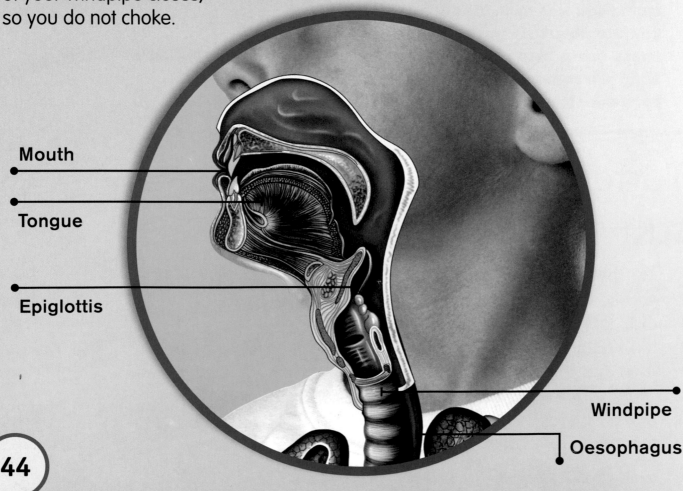

Mouth

Tongue

Epiglottis

Windpipe

Oesophagus

# Stretchy bag

Your stomach lies inside your ribcage. It is like a stretchy bag that expands to hold your meal. Muscles in the stomach wall mix food into a pulp. The stomach lining releases powerful chemicals, which dissolve food and make it mushy.

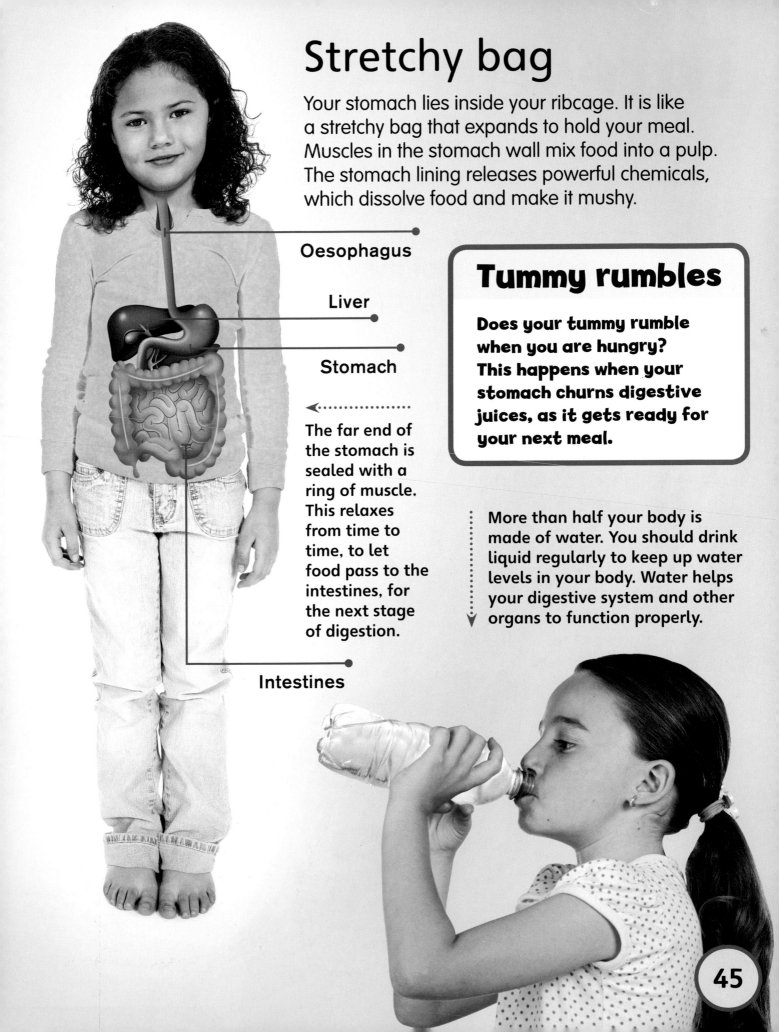

Oesophagus

Liver

Stomach

The far end of the stomach is sealed with a ring of muscle. This relaxes from time to time, to let food pass to the intestines, for the next stage of digestion.

Intestines

## Tummy rumbles

Does your tummy rumble when you are hungry? This happens when your stomach churns digestive juices, as it gets ready for your next meal.

More than half your body is made of water. You should drink liquid regularly to keep up water levels in your body. Water helps your digestive system and other organs to function properly.

45

# Intestines

Half-digested food from your stomach passes into your intestines, which finish the work of digestion. Your intestines are a very long tube, divided into two parts: the small intestine and the large intestine. Most of the goodness in your food passes into your body, through the intestines.

## Small intestine

Your small intestine is lined with thousands of very small finger-shaped parts called villi. These contain tiny blood vessels. Goodness from your food passes though the villi walls into your bloodstream. The blood carries it away to where it is needed.

Your small intestine coils around inside the lower part of your body, below your ribcage.

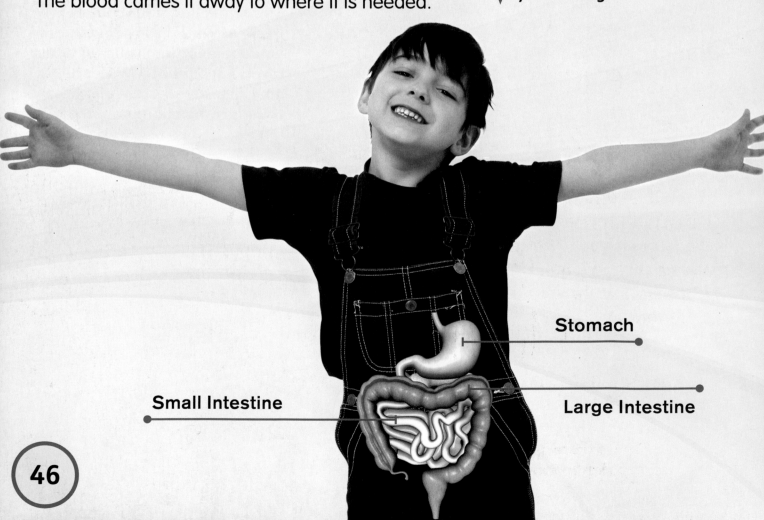

Stomach

Small Intestine

Large Intestine

# Liver and pancreas

Your liver and pancreas help with digestion. They supply powerful juices, which dissolve (break down) food in the intestines. Your liver also stores nutrients (goodness) until your body needs them for energy.

## Small and large

**Your small intestine is 6 metres (20 feet) long. It is over five times as long as your large intestine. But your large intestine is much wider.**

Your liver stores sugars that give you energy to be active even when you haven't eaten for a while.

# Large intestine

Your large intestine is shorter and wider than your small intestine. Here, nutrients and water pass into your blood. The waste food that is left behind gets more and more solid. Finally, the leftover waste passes into the rectum, where it is stored until you go to the toilet. This waste comes out as poo.

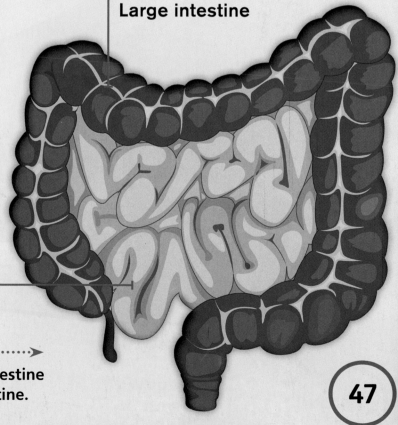

Large intestine

Small intestine

**This picture shows the large intestine looping around the small intestine.**

47

# Body Wastes

All animals produce waste, including you. There are two main types of waste: solid and liquid waste. Liquid, called pee or urine, is mainly waste water from the blood. Solid waste, called poo or faeces, is waste material from food.

## Cleaning the blood

Your kidneys filter and clean your blood. Waste water from your kidneys passes down two tubes called ureters into a hollow organ called the bladder. The bladder stretches like a balloon to hold the liquid until you go to the toilet.

..............................................➤

**Your kidneys are two bean-shaped organs. They lie on either side of your spine, at the back, just below your waist.**

**Kidney**

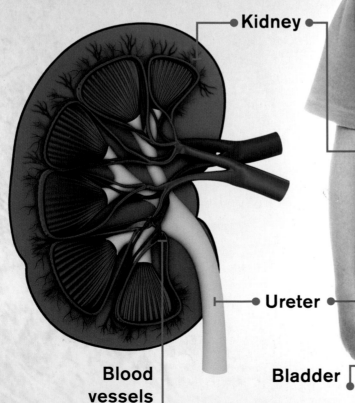

**Ureter**

**Blood vessels**

**Bladder**

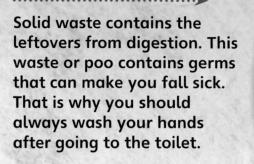

Solid waste contains the leftovers from digestion. This waste or poo contains germs that can make you fall sick. That is why you should always wash your hands after going to the toilet.

# Waste gases

Your body also produces waste gases. Waste air passes out of your lungs. Waste gases from your digestive system pass out of your mouth when you burp, or out of your bottom. This is a natural part of digestion.

Foods containing lots of fibre help you digest your food.

# Fibre

Solid waste is mostly fibre. But you need to eat lots of fibre to keep your digestive system working properly. Foods such as wholemeal bread, cereal and green vegetables have lots of fibre.

# The Five Senses

The five main senses are sight, smell, hearing, touch and taste. What you know about the world comes from sense organs such as your eyes, nose, ears, skin and tongue.

These sense organs send messages to your brain. Most sense organs are found on your head, but the sense of touch comes from your skin, which covers your whole body.

**Your five senses help you to enjoy a visit to the seaside.**

Sight and smell allow you to enjoy flowers.

The sense of taste allows you to enjoy ice lollies.

The sense of touch allows you to feel gritty sand between your toes. Your sense of hearing lets you enjoy the cries of gulls.

# Eyes and Seeing

Sight is the most important sense for most people. You use your eyes to see where you are going, to catch a ball, to spot your friends and to eat and drink without spilling things. Sight is also important for learning and for reading this book.

## Eye parts

Look in a mirror. The coloured part of your eye is called the iris. In the centre is a hole called the pupil. This lets light into your eye. In dim light, your pupils get bigger to let in more light. In bright light, they get smaller, so you don't get dazzled.

Your eyes are set in bony sockets that protect them from knocks and scratches. Your eyebrows and eyelashes help to keep out dirt and sweat. If something does get in, your eyes water to wash it out.

# How do you see?

Light enters your eye through the pupil. The iris is the coloured part of your eye. It controls how much light enters by expanding or shrinking the pupil. Light passes through the lens, which focuses it on a light-sensitive area at the back called the retina. This area sends signals to the brain. The brain tells you what you see.

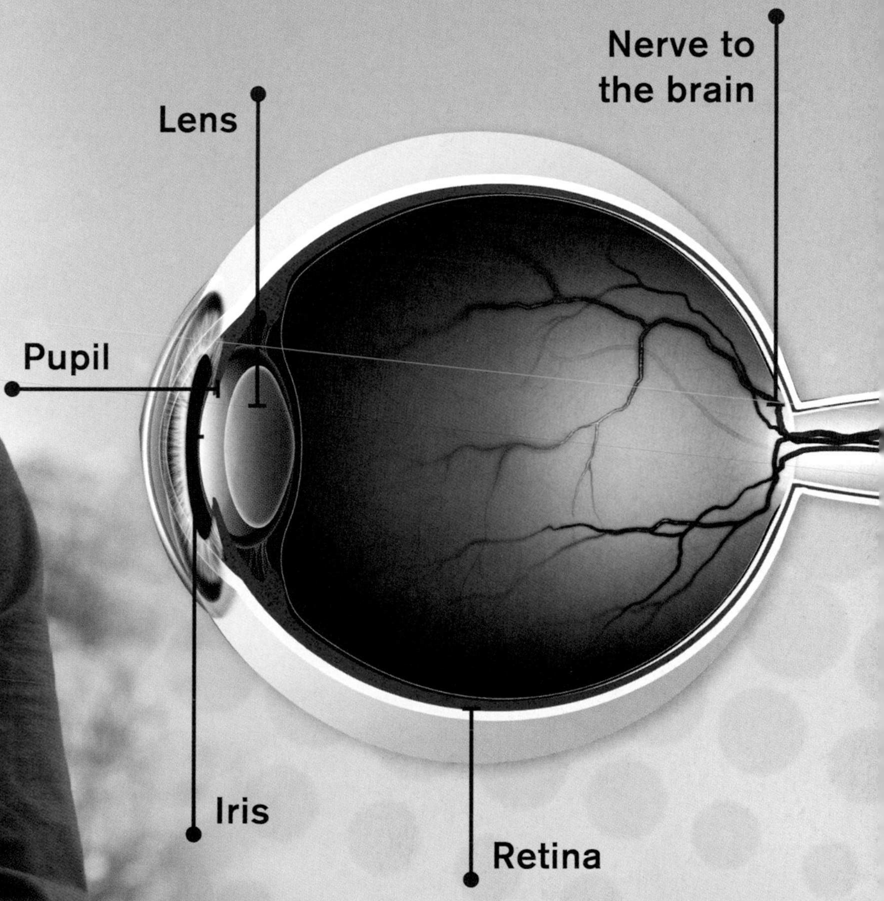

Nerve to the brain

Lens

Pupil

Iris

Retina

This picture shows the inside of the eye.

Your eyes are several centimetres apart. Each eye sees a slightly different view. Your brain sorts out the signals from each eye. This allows you to judge distances and to catch a ball.

# Touch and Hearing

Your ears pick up all sorts of noises such as faint sounds from far away and loud sounds from things close by. You can hear high sounds such as the squeak of a mouse, or low sounds such as the growl of a dog. Your skin gives you the sense of touch. When your skin touches something, it tells you if that thing is hot or cold, hard or soft.

## Sensitive skin

Your skin is your largest organ. It covers the whole of your body, from top to toe. All over your skin are sensors that are joined to a nerve. When you touch something, the sensor sends signals to the brain to tell you what it feels like.

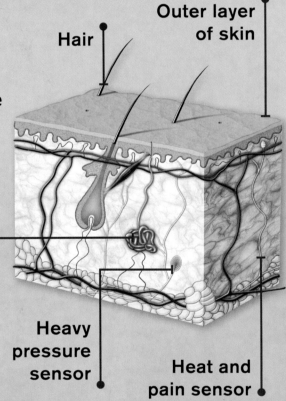

Hair

Outer layer of skin

Light touch sensor

Heavy pressure sensor

Heat and pain sensor

▲ This picture shows a close-up of the skin. Some touch sensors are near the surface, others are deeper in the skin.

◄ Sensors in your skin tell you whether something, such as this cat, is hard or soft, rough or smooth. Other sensors in your skin tell you if you are sore, itchy or in pain.

# How do you hear?

Your outer ear channels sounds into your ear. When the sounds hit the tightly stretched eardrum, it wobbles. Ripples pass through the tiny bones of the middle ear to the snail-shaped cochlea. This sends signals to the brain. Your ears also help you balance. Three tiny loops called semi-circular canals are filled with liquid. When you move your head, this liquid swirls. This sends signals to your brain about the position of your head.

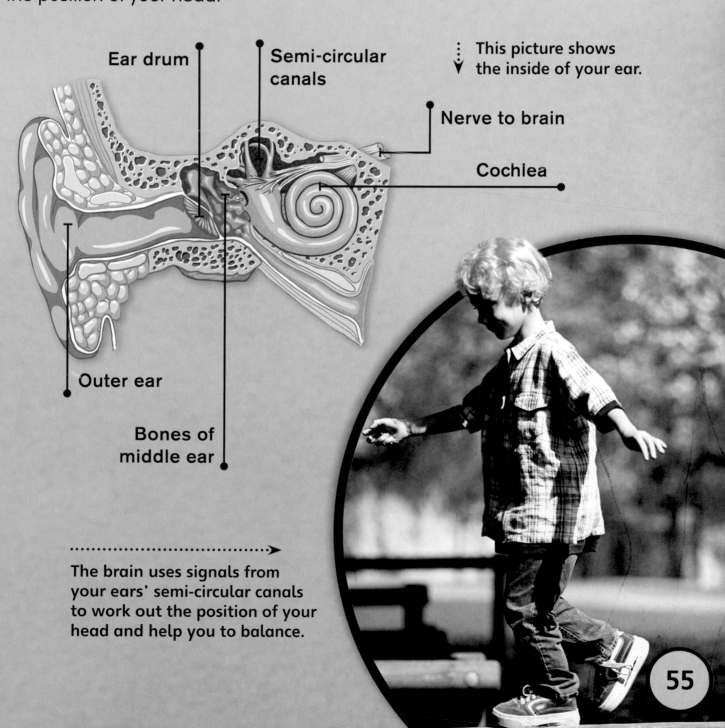

## Different shapes

No two people's ears are exactly the same shape.

Ear drum

Semi-circular canals

⋮
↓ This picture shows the inside of your ear.

Nerve to brain

Cochlea

Outer ear

Bones of middle ear

•••••••••••••••••••••••→

The brain uses signals from your ears' semi-circular canals to work out the position of your head and help you to balance.

# Smell and Taste

Your senses of smell and taste help you to enjoy your favourite food. They also warn you of things that can be dangerous, such as the smell of burning, or of rotten food. Things that smell and taste good are usually safe to eat.

## How do we smell?

A freshly baked loaf gives off a delicious smell in the air. Smells floating in the air enter your nostrils. They reach a space, like a little cave, called the nasal cavity. On the roof of the cave are smell sensors, which send messages to the brain. Your brain sorts out these signals.

**Smell-sensing area**

**Nasal cavity**

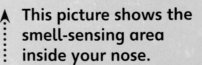
This picture shows the smell-sensing area inside your nose.

# Sweet and salty

The surface of your tongue is covered with thousands of tiny bumps called papillae, which contain taste sensors. We call them taste buds. Your tongue can identify four main tastes: sweet, sour, salty and bitter.

◄········································

The bumps on your tongue help it to grip onto slippery food such as a lolly. Taste buds also help you to tell if food is tasting right or not. That's why you spit out spoiled milk as soon as you taste it.

## Amazing senses

There are about 10,000 taste buds on your tongue. Your nose can also smell about 10,000 different scents! Smell and taste are closely linked. If you have a cold or a blocked nose, you'll find that your food doesn't taste as good.

········································►

Each of your taste buds contains 50 to 100 cells that can pick up sweet, sour, salty and bitter tastes. They can also pick up a fifth taste called "umami" (Japanese for "pleasant tasting") which comes from certain flavourings used in food.

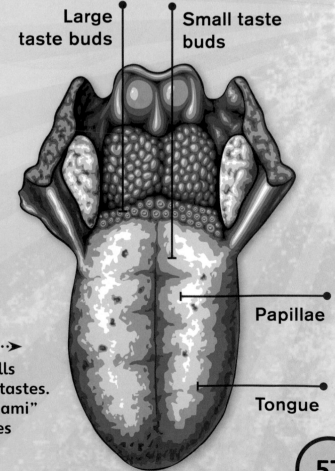

Large taste buds

Small taste buds

Papillae

Tongue

# Birth and Growing

Your life began even before you were born. You spent nine months growing inside your mother. After you were born, you grew from a baby into a toddler, then a child. Before many years have passed you will be a teenager, then a grown-up.

Our bodies grow and change while we are children and teenagers. When we are adults we stop growing but our bodies carry on changing.

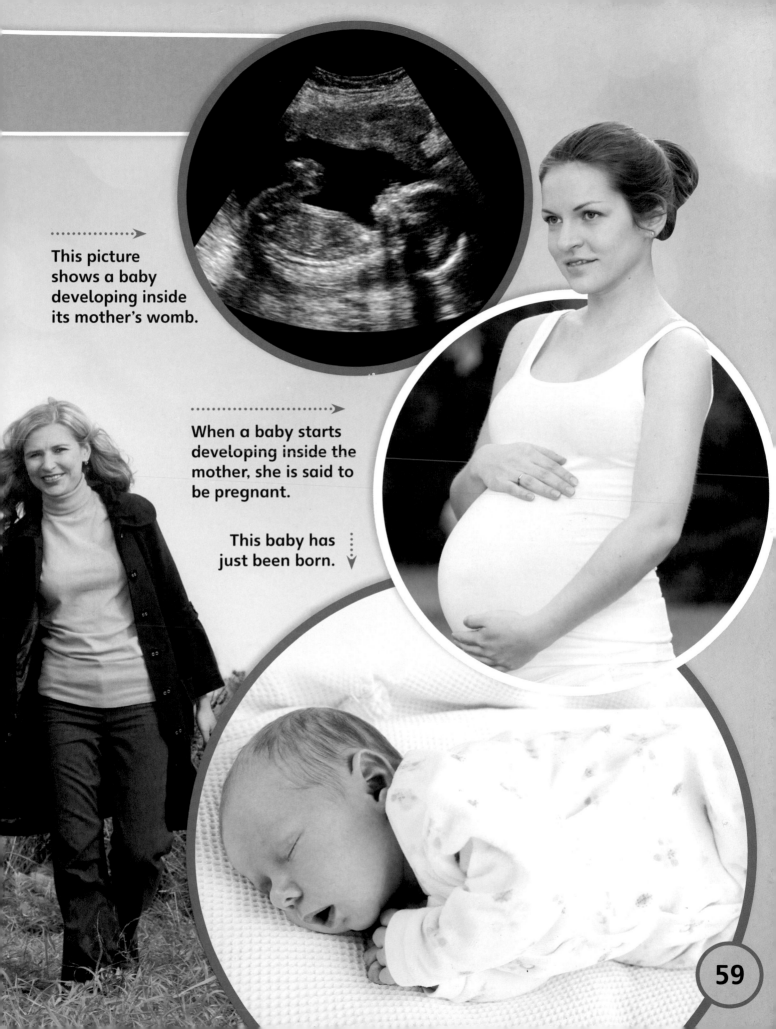

This picture shows a baby developing inside its mother's womb.

When a baby starts developing inside the mother, she is said to be pregnant.

This baby has just been born.

# How Life Begins

A new human life begins when an egg cell from a woman joins with a sperm cell from a man. The woman becomes pregnant and soon she will be a mother. Before you were born, you began growing inside your mother's tummy, in a space called the womb.

## Sperm and egg join

Sperm cells swim towards the egg cell inside the mother. One sperm joins with the egg to make it fertile. This cell will develop into a baby.

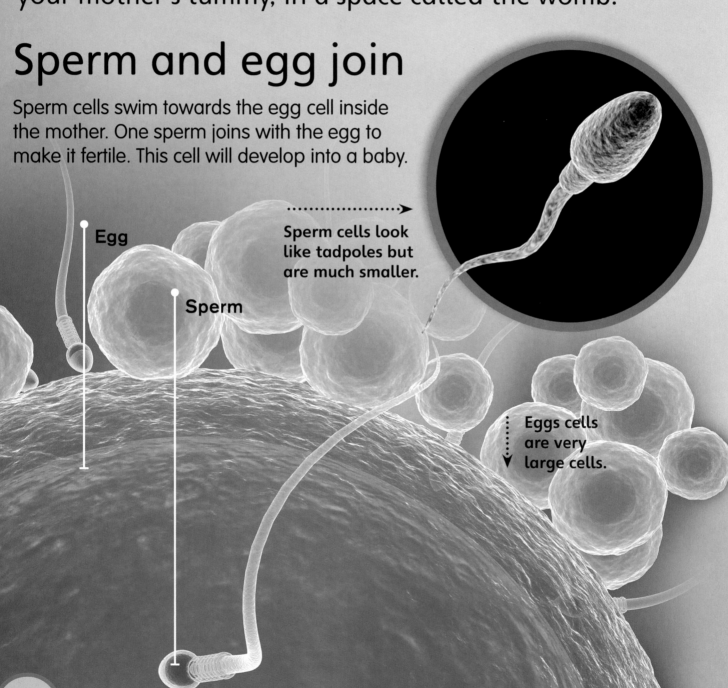

Egg

Sperm

Sperm cells look like tadpoles but are much smaller.

Eggs cells are very large cells.

# Cells divide

The fertile egg cell divides to make two cells. These divide again to make four cells, then eight, 16 and so on. Five days later, there is a ball of about 100 cells. This settles in the soft lining of the mother's womb and carries on developing.

An unborn baby at four weeks looks a little like a tadpole. Over the next few weeks, the baby's cells carry on dividing and quite soon there are thousands, then millions of cells. Cells of the same type group together to build body parts such as the brain, heart and lungs.

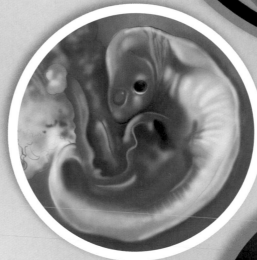

This picture shows a cluster of eggs dividing.

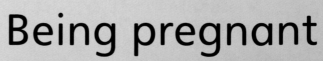

At eight weeks old, the baby has all the main body parts, including eyes and ears. It also has arms and legs, fingers and toes, but it is still very tiny.

# Being pregnant

A woman is said to be pregnant when a baby starts developing inside her. Her tummy gets bigger as the baby grows inside her. When the unborn baby is about 20 weeks old, the mother can feel it kicking, as it exercises its muscles.

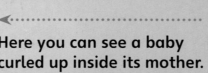

Here you can see a baby curled up inside its mother.

# Before You Were Born

You began life in your mother's womb as a tiny cell, about as big as a grain of sand. But as the weeks went by, you grew and developed very quickly. You began to look like a baby. After nine months, you were ready to be born.

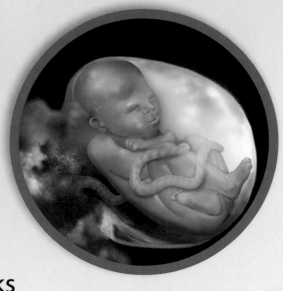

An unborn baby develops in the womb inside a bag filled with liquid. Inside the womb it is dark, warm, quiet and safe.

## Growing in the womb

Before you were born, you could not breathe or feed yourself. Oxygen and nutrients (goodness) from your mother's blood passed through a tube called the umbilical cord into your body. Your belly button marks the place where this tube was attached.

These pictures show a baby developing inside its mother's womb.

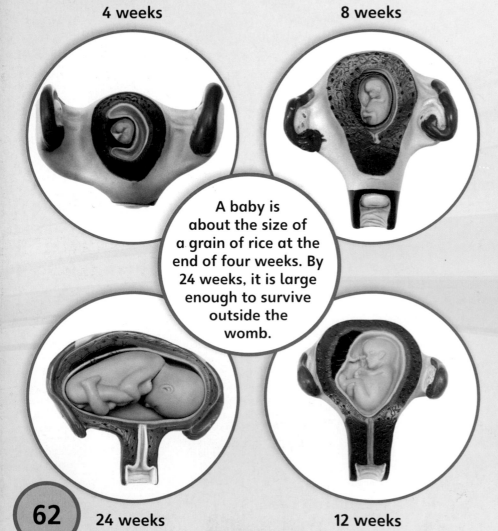

**4 weeks**

**8 weeks**

A baby is about the size of a grain of rice at the end of four weeks. By 24 weeks, it is large enough to survive outside the womb.

**24 weeks**

**12 weeks**

# Birth

After about 38 weeks in your mother's womb, you were ready to be born. Muscles in the walls of the womb tightened to squeeze you down a tube called the birth canal, which is between your mother's legs. You squeezed through and were born. A nurse or doctor cut the umbilical cord that joined you to your mother.

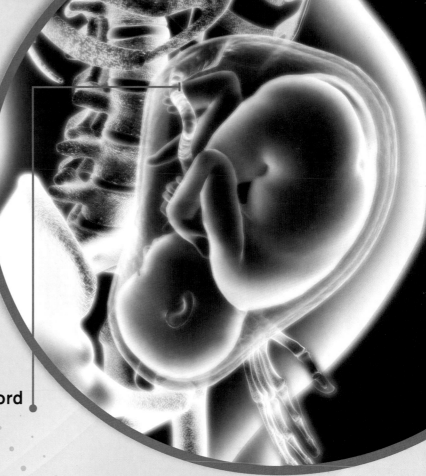

**Umbilical cord**

Just before birth, most babies turn around, so they are upside down. That way the baby is born easily, head-first.

# Breast feeding

Newborn babies drink milk. They cannot eat solid food. Most newborn babies drink their mother's breast milk. At the age of about four to six months babies can begin to eat solid food.

**Your first food was milk, from your mother or a bottle.**

63

# Growing Older

Have you seen photos of yourself when you were a baby and a toddler? Photographs help to remind you how much your body changes each year. As you grow into an adult, you get taller. Other body changes continue as you get older.

## Baby

As soon as you were born, you felt cool air around you and heard loud sounds for the first time. You could not talk, but you knew how to cry when you were hungry.

## Toddler

As babies wave their arms and legs, their muscles get stronger. By about six months old you could hold your head up and sit up. By about nine months you were probably crawling.

## Child

An eight-year-old child has many skills. You can read, write and do maths. You may be able to swim, ride a bike and play a musical instrument. You are also getting taller and stronger.

# Teenager

Teenagers grow quickly. Between the ages of 11 and 15, your body changes a lot as you start to become an adult. This time is called puberty.

# Adult

By the age of about 20, your body is fully grown. You are a "grown-up", and able to take care of yourself and others properly.

# Getting older

After 20 years of age, your body starts to age slowly. Your skin starts to wrinkle. After the age of 50 years, your sight and hearing may not be so good.

# Keeping Healthy

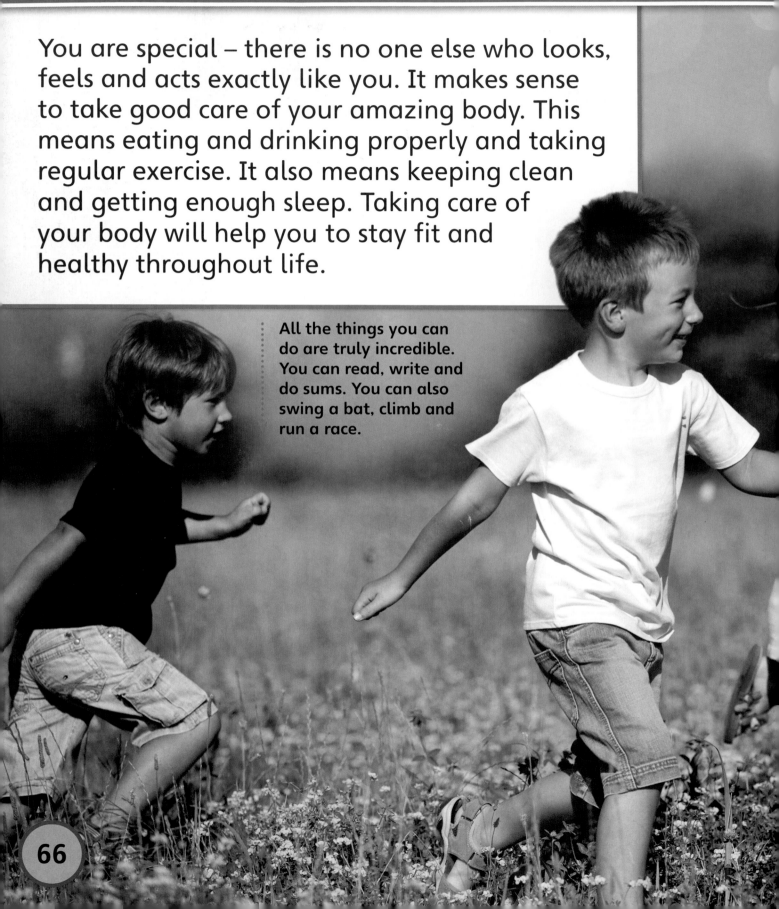

You are special – there is no one else who looks, feels and acts exactly like you. It makes sense to take good care of your amazing body. This means eating and drinking properly and taking regular exercise. It also means keeping clean and getting enough sleep. Taking care of your body will help you to stay fit and healthy throughout life.

All the things you can do are truly incredible. You can read, write and do sums. You can also swing a bat, climb and run a race.

You must rest when you are ill so that your body can recover and repair itself.

Keep clean by bathing or showering regularly.

Eating healthy food will keep your body in tip-top condition.

# Why Do I Get Ill?

Tiny living things called germs are everywhere and can make you ill. Luckily, your body is able to fight off germs to make you well again. Your skin and the white cells in your blood are important body parts for keeping healthy.

## Germs

Most germs are harmless, but two main types can make you ill. These are bacteria and viruses. Germs are all around you – in the air, in the soil and on animals. If you eat food you have touched with dirty hands, you can get ill. That's why you need to wash your hands after you touch animals or dirt and after you go to the bathroom.

**This picture shows a white blood cell surrounding and eating a germ. Germs are far too tiny to see with your eyes. This picture was taken using a microscope.**

Your skin keeps germs from entering your body, but they can get in through cuts and grazes. Wash a wound thoroughly to get rid of germs. Then cover it with a clean plaster.

# Colds and flu

Are you feeling poorly? With a sore throat or runny nose? You may have a cold. If you have a high temperature, it could be flu. Both colds and flu are caused by viruses. You will need to rest in bed and drink lots of liquid. This will give your body a chance to make white blood cells to beat the germs.

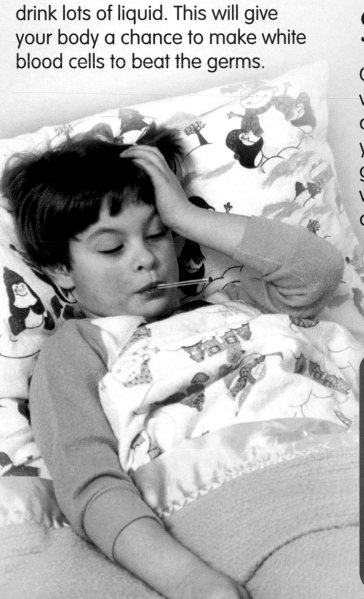

# Spreading germs

Colds and flu are mainly spread by viruses floating in the air. When you cough or sneeze, you blast germs out of your nose and mouth. Avoid spreading germs by covering your nose and mouth with your hand or a tissue when you cough or sneeze.

You should rest at home if you have a fever. If you go to school, your germs could make others sick, too.

## Vaccinations

A vaccine is a harmless version of a germ which a nurse gives to you as an injection. This helps your body prepare for when a real germ of the same type attacks.

69

# Healthy Eating

Food gives you energy to keep going, and the nutrients you need to grow and repair your body. You need to eat lots of different foods to keep your body healthy. You should also drink plenty of water.

## Eating well

A healthy diet includes carbohydrates, proteins, plenty of fresh fruit and vegetables and a little fat. Try not to eat too much of any one food.

## Carbohydrates

Carbohydrates give you energy. Bread, rice, potatoes, pasta and cereal all contain carbohydrates. These foods release plenty of energy to keep you going.

## Proteins

Your body needs protein to grow and repair cells. Fish, meat, cheese and beans contain protein. Cheese and milk also contain calcium, which makes your bones strong.

A healthy diet includes carbohydrates like pasta (above), proteins like eggs, cheese, meat and fish (right) as well as fruit and vegetables.

# Fruit and vegetables

Fresh fruit and vegetables provide vitamins, minerals and fibre to keep you healthy. Beans, cereals and wholemeal bread contain fibre, too.

The fibre in vegetables and fruit helps your body to digest food.

# Fats

Your body needs a little fat to keep your nerves healthy. Dairy foods, nuts, meat and fish all contain good fats. Too many fatty foods, such as cakes, crisps and chocolate, are bad for you.

## Watery world

An amazing two-thirds of your body is water. You lose water when you sweat, breathe and go to the toilet. You need to drink a lot of liquid every day to replace the water you lose.

# Looking After Your Body

Your skin, hair, teeth and nails are the main features on the outside of your body. They are also the first things people see when they look at you. You should take good care of them, like the rest of your body.

## Skin

Skin is your body's outer layer. It helps to protect important organs and keeps out germs. It also controls your body temperature by sweating and shivering. Too much sun damages your skin and makes it wrinkly.

When you go out on sunny days, always put on sun cream. You can also put on a hat to help protect your skin.

## Special material

Your hair and nails are made of a material called keratin. A rhino's horn and a bird's beak and claws are also made of keratin.

# Nails

Your fingernails and toenails protect your sensitive fingers and toes. Dirt and germs can get under your nails. If you touch food with dirty hands, the germs can make you ill. Keep your nails short and scrubbed clean.

# Hair

**Wash your hands after going to the toilet and before you touch food.**

You have two types of hair – coarse hair on your head, eyebrows and eyelashes, and fine hair on your body. Hair helps to keep your body warm. Washing your hair with shampoo removes dirt and oil. Regular brushing makes your hair shiny.

**Brush your hair regularly to remove any tangles.**

# Keeping clean

Every day you get dirty and sweaty. Dirt carries germs and stale sweat can make you smell. Wash with soap and water and brush your teeth twice a day to keep them healthy.

**Bathing and washing your hair regularly keeps you smelling sweet.**

# Staying Fit

A fit body is a healthy body. Regular exercise helps keep your body in top condition. It helps you to stay at the right weight and keeps your mind alert, too. Eating the right foods and getting enough sleep also keep your body healthy.

## Exercise

Doing exercise strengthens your muscles and bones and keeps you supple (bendy). Exercise that makes you breathe fast is good for your heart and lungs. Try to play sport, swim, dance or go for a run or a bike ride at least three times a week.

Exercise in the fresh air is fun and makes you feel good. Swimming builds stamina, so you can keep going for longer. Swinging on bars in the playground builds strong bones and muscles.

# Warming up and cooling down

Stretching and bending before you exercise warms your muscles and makes joints supple. When you finish exercising you will be hot and sweaty. Drink liquids and put on a sweater so you do not get chilly as you cool down. Have a good wash later, too.

**Dancing makes you supple and builds your stamina. Stretch before you start.**

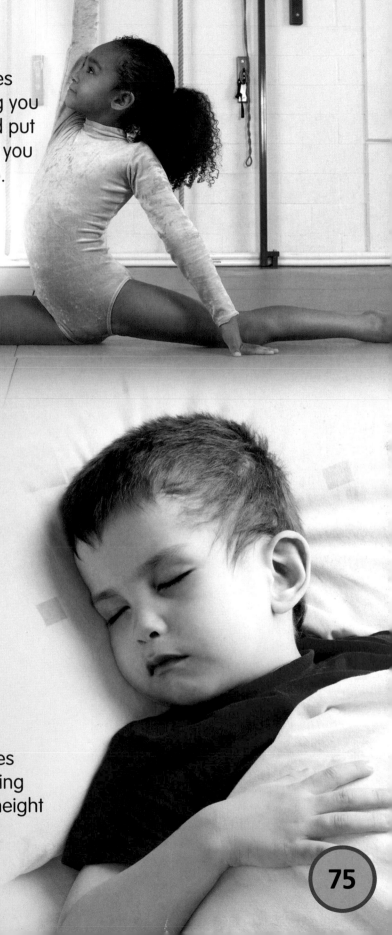

# Sleep

Sleep is especially important when you are growing. You grow fastest when you are asleep. When you start yawning, it is time to go to bed.

**A newborn baby sleeps for about 20 hours a day. An eight-year-old child needs about ten hours of sleep. Adults sleep for about seven to eight hours a day.**

# Check-ups

A regular check-up by your doctor makes sure you are growing properly and staying healthy. Your doctor will measure your height and weight. You should have your teeth checked regularly by a dentist, too.

# Useful Words

**arteries**  Blood vessels that carry blood away from your heart.

**birth canal**  The passage between a woman's legs through which a baby passes to be born.

**blood vessels**  The tubes through which blood flows.

**bone marrow**  A jelly in the centre of bones, which makes blood cells.

**brain stem**  Part of your brain that controls processes such as breathing and digestion.

**bronchi**  The main airways that lead from your windpipe to your lungs.

**capillaries**  Tiny blood vessels running between arteries and veins.

**cartilage**  The rubbery substance which forms your outer ear and nose. Cartilage also coats the ends of bones at joints.

**cells**  The tiny units from which living things are made.

**cerebellum**  The part of your brain that helps with balance and coordination.

**cerebrum**  The wrinkled top part of your brain. You use your cerebrum to think.

**cochlea**  A coiled tube in your inner ear which allows you to hear.

**diaphragm**  The large, flat muscle at the base of your lungs, which is used in breathing.

**digestion**  When food is broken down and the nourishment (goodness) it contains becomes part of your body.

**fertile**  Capable of producing a baby.

**joints**  The places where two bones meet.

**keratin**  A tough material found in skin, hair and nails.

**kidneys**  The organs that clean and filter blood.

**ligaments**  Tough bands that hold bones in place at a joint.

**liver**  An organ that does many important jobs. It stores nutrients and cleans the blood.

**mucus**  A sticky fluid, made in the lining of your airways, which traps dust and dirt.

**muscle fibres**  The long, thin cells inside skeletal muscles that get shorter to pull on bones.

**nasal cavity**  A hollow space which leads from your nostrils to your throat.

**nerves**  The long, thin fibres that carry signals to and from your brain.

**nutrients**  The nourishment (goodness) in food.

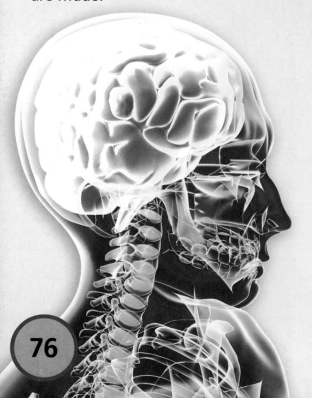

**stethoscope** An instrument that doctors use to hear sounds in your body, such as the beating of your heart.

**taste buds** The tiny sensors on your tongue, cheeks or throat that pick up flavours in food, and allow you to taste.

**tendons** The long, stringy cords that join muscles to bones.

**urine** Liquid waste.

**veins** Large blood vessels that carry blood to your heart.

**vertebrae** The small, knobbly bones that make up your spine.

**villi** Tiny finger-shaped parts inside your small intestine. They help the intestine to absorb nutrients.

**vocal cords** Two stretchy flaps in your windpipe that move to produce sound.

**womb** The part of a woman where a baby develops.

**oesophagus** The pipe that carries food and drink to your stomach.

**pancreas** An organ that makes digestive juices.

**plasma** The liquid part of blood.

**platelets** Tiny blood cells which help your blood to clot.

**puberty** The time of growth during which your body changes from a child to an adult.

**pulse** The feel of your heart's beat as it pumps blood around your body.

**retina** A light-sensitive area in the back of your eye, that sends visual information to your brain.

**semi-circular canals** The three fluid-filled loops in your inner ear that help you to balance.

**skeleton** Your body's framework, which is made mainly of bone.

**sperm** A cell from a man which joins with a woman's egg to make a baby.

**spinal cord** The body's main nerve, which links your brain with smaller nerves throughout your body.

# Index

# Picture Credits

t=top, c=centre, b=bottom, tr=top right, tl=top left, tc=top centre, cr=centre right, cl=centre left, br=bottom right, bl=bottom left.

**Cover:** © **Shutterstock.com:** Milos Stojiljkovic

**Title Page**: © **Shutterstock.com:** Milos Stojiljkovic

**Half Title**: © **Shutterstock.com:** Milos Stojiljkovic

**Contents Page**: **Bigstock**: Sebastian Kaulitzki, Sebastian Kaulitzki, Arvind Balaraman, Alexander Raths; **Thinkstock:** Hemera

**Inside**:

**Bigstock:** Vasyl Yakobchuk P7(c); Joanna Zieli P7(b); Sebastian Kaulitzki P8-9; Arvind Balaraman P10(l); Sebastian Kaulitzki P10(r); Sebastian Kaulitzki P11(b); Bram Janssens P12-13; Alexander Raths P13(t); Ints Tomsons P14; Daniel Kaesler P15(t); Juan Carlos Tinjaca P18(t); Sebastian Kaulitzki P18(t); Sebastian Kaulitzki P19(b); Stjepan Banovic P22(l); Sebastian Kaulitzki P23(cl); Pavel Losevsky P23(b); Patrick Hermans P24(r); Olga Aleksandrovna Lisitskaya P25(tl); Andrea Danti P29(t); Sebastian Kaulitzki P29(b), P30, P34(tr); Rhonda ODonnell P31(b); Sebastian Kaulitzki P32 (t); Ryan Pike P34(cl); Sebastian Kaulitzki P35; Yuri Arcurs P36(t); Sebastian Kaulitzki P36(t), P37(b); Pavel Losevsky P38(cl), P40; Susan Leggett P41(b); Linda Bucklin P42(r); Nguyet M Le P43(t); Yuri Arcurs P45(l); Matt Cole P47(b); Sebastian Kaulitzki P48(l); Juan Carlos Tinjaca, Sebastian Kaulitzki P48(r); Gorilla P49(t); Arvind Balaraman P51(t); Vinicius Ramalho Tupinamba P51(c); Andrea Danti P54(r); Oguz Aral P55(l); Leonello Calvetti P56(b); Kirill Zdorov P57(t); Oguz Aral P57(b); Sebastian Kaulitzki P60-61; Pakhay Oleksandr P67(tl); Leah-Anne Thompson P67(c); Celso Pupo Rodrigues P70(b); Cathy Yeulet P71(t); Sebastian Kaulitzki P76; **Fotolia**: Jacek Chabraszewski P22(r); 3Drenderings P46; Microimages P55(b); Godfer P65(t); **iStockphoto**: SergiyN P24(r); Alexander Kozachok P60(cr); Dmitry Knorre P61(tr); **Science Photo Library**: Susumu Nishinaga/Science Photo Library P33(t); 3D4Medical.Com/ Science Photo Library P34(cr); Clouds Hill Imaging Ltd/Science Photo Library P34(br); M. Dauenheimer, Custom Medical Stock Photo/Science Photo Library P37(t); Jacopin/Science Photo Library P38(cr), P38(br); Medi-Mation/ Science Photo Library P63(t); P68; **Shutterstock**: Chris Harvey P30; Blamb P31(t); Sorin Popa P62(b); **Thinkstock**: Comstock P6-7; Jupiterimages/Brand X Pictures P7(t); Jupiterimages/Pixland P9(t); iStockphoto P9(b); iStockphoto P11(t); Jupiterimages/Comstock/Getty Images P11(c); Jeff Randall/Digital Vision P15(b); iStockphoto P16; iStockphoto P17(t); Hemera P17(cl); Hemera P17(cr); Comstock P17(b); Jupiterimages/ Goodshoot/Getty Images P19(t); iStockphoto 19(c); Hemera P21(t); iStockphoto P21(b); iStockphoto P23(t); iStockphoto P23(c); Stockbyte P25(tr); Stockbyte P27(l); Comstock P27(r); Hemera P28-29; Stockbyte P29(c); Stockbyte P30, P31(c); Hemera P32(b); Stockbyte P33(b); Digital Vision P39(t); Comstock P39(b); Digital Vision P41(t); Hemera P41(c); iStockphoto P42(l), P43(b); Hemera P44, P45(r), P46; Brand X Pictures P47(t); iStockphoto P49(c); Goodshoot P49(b); Digital Vision P50-51; iStockphoto P51(b); Comstock P52; Polka Dot P53(l); iStockphoto P54(l); Valueline P56(t); Hemera P58-59, P59(t); iStockphoto P59(c); BananaStock P59(b); Hemera P63(b), P64(tl), P64(cl), P64(br); Stockbyte P65(c); Photodisc P65(b); iStockphoto P66-67, P78; Stockbyte P67(b); Comstock P69(t); Liquidlibrary P69(b); Hemera P70(t); Photodisc P70(b); Hemera P71(b); Stockbyte P72; Hemera P73(t), P73(cl), P73(br); iStockphoto P74(l), P74(c), P74(r); BananaStock P75(t); Hemera P75(b), P77(t); **Q2AMedia Art Bank**: P9(l), P12, P13(l), P18, P20, P24(l), P25(b), P26, P36(b), P44, P45(l), P53(r), P61(l), P62, P77(b).